Monika Bremicker

Lehrerhandreichung:
Kopiervorlagen zu
Rosso,
The Australian Connection
und
Betrayed

Cornelsen

Inhalt

Lehrerhandreichung:
Kopiervorlagen zu
Rosso, The Australian Connection
und *Betrayed*

Monika Bremicker

Redaktion
Neil Porter

*Gestaltung und
technische Umsetzung*
Manuela Tanner

Illustration
Gabriele Heinisch

http://www.cornelsen.de

1. Auflage €
Druck 7 6 5 4
Jahr 08 07 06 05

© 1999 Cornelsen Verlag, Berlin

Das Werk und seine Teile sind urheberrechtlich geschützt. Jede Nutzung in anderen als den gesetzlich zugelassenen Fällen bedarf der vorherigen schriftlichen Einwilligung des Verlages. Hinweis zu § 52a UrhG: Weder das Werk noch seine Teile dürfen ohne eine solche Einwilligung eingescannt und in ein Netzwerk eingestellt werden. Dies gilt auch für Intranets von Schulen und sonstigen Bildungseinrichtungen. Die Kopiervorlagen dürfen für den eigenen Unterrichtsgebrauch in der jeweils benötigten Anzahl vervielfältigt werden.

Druck: Druckhaus Berlin-Mitte

ISBN 3-464-6818-8

Bestellnummer 68188

Gedruckt auf Recyclingpapier,
hergestellt aus 100% Altpapier.

Vorwort	3
Worksheets	
Rosso	4
The Australian Connection	22
Betrayed	34
Solutions to the worksheets	
Rosso	54
The Australian Connection	62
Betrayed	69

Vorwort

„Und nach der nächsten Unit lesen wir eine Lektüre." Endlich eine Abwechslung von der ständig gleichen Lehrwerkroutine – dafür sind Schüler wie Lehrer dankbar. Für die Lernenden stellt das Lesen und Verstehen eines längeren englischen Textes ein Erfolgserlebnis dar. Sie merken, was sie schon in der Fremdsprache erreicht haben, und haben auch noch Spaß an spannenden Inhalten, die im Unterricht behandelte Sachthemen häufig durch eine interessante Spielhandlung vertiefen und durch eine neue Perspektive in einem anderen Licht erscheinen lassen.

Damit die Schüler wirklich mit Freude und Interesse bei der Sache sind, ist es wesentlich, Texte auszuwählen, die sprachlich nicht zu schwierig sind, nicht durch viele unbekannte Wörter oder Strukturen den Lesefluss hemmen. Auch ist es wichtig, durch abwechslungsreiche Übungen, Fragen, Rätsel usw. das Textverständnis zu sichern, den Wortschatz zu erweitern und Redeanlässe zu schaffen. Diese Aufgabe soll der vorliegende Lehrerbegleitband erfüllen. Er bietet ein reichhaltiges Angebot an diversen Aufgaben, die zur Beschäftigung mit der jeweiligen Lektüre anregen. Er ist nicht so zu verstehen, dass jedes Arbeitsblatt „abgearbeitet" werden soll. Vielmehr ist es dem Lehrer überlassen, eine auf die jeweilige Lerngruppe und -situation abgestimmte Auswahl zu treffen. Das Material sollte aber eine wesentliche Hilfe bei der Unterrichtsvorbereitung und -durchführung darstellen.

Für den vorliegenden Band wurden drei Lektüren der Cornelsen English Library ausgewählt, die im Anspruchsniveau durchaus unterschiedlich sind. Sprachlich am einfachsten und auch inhaltlich für jüngere Schüler geeignet ist *Rosso*. Etwas schwieriger und für eine höhere Klasse geeignet ist *The Australian Connection*, ein Text, den man im Anschluss an eine Australien-Unit im Lehrwerk behandeln kann. Das höchste Anspruchsniveau der hier aufgenommenen Texte hat *Betrayed*, eine Geschichte, die vielfältige Rede- und Diskussionsanlässe bietet.

Die Arbeitsblätter sind konzipiert als Kopiervorlagen, die unmittelbar im Unterricht eingesetzt werden können. Bei den mit einem ◐ versehenen Übungsteilen können die Schüler die Lösungen in das Arbeitsblatt eintragen. Die mit einem ✪ gekennzeichneten Aufgaben erfordern mehr Schreibraum und sollen im Heft bearbeitet werden.

Viel Erfolg beim Einsatz im Unterricht!

Monika Bremicker

Worksheets Ch. 1

A. Collect all the information you can find about Rosso and make a mind-map based on the one below:

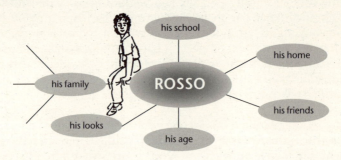

Now make a mind-map of Julia.

B. Answer the following questions.

1. Why is Rosso different from the other boys and girls at his school?

2. Why is he often very lonely?

3. Why does Rosso's mother not take him with her when she is working?

4. Do Jake and Rosso often talk about Rosso's father?

5. What are Jake's plans for Rosso's future? ▷ _____

_____

_____

6. Why did Rosso buy a big red notebook one day? ▷ _____

_____

_____

_____

7. Who is Julia? ▷ _____

_____

_____

C. Find the words in the text for the following:

1. a vehicle you can live in:

   ▷ _____

2. when you have nobody to talk to you are

   ▷ _____

3. a place where people put things that they do not need any longer

   ▷ _____

4. the money you get for your work

   ▷ _____

5. a place where you keep a car

   ▷ _____

Worksheets — Ch. 2

▶ **A. Some questions on the text:**

1. Why hadn't Julia wanted to move to London? ▷ _____

2. What kind of place is Battersea? ▷ _____

3. What did she like about Rosso on her first day at school? ▷ _____

4. Why did Julia look for Culvert Place? ▷ _____

5. How did Rosso treat her in the street and at school? ▷ _____

6. Can you explain his behaviour? ▷ _____

▶ **B. What subjects did Rosso and Julia have on the day they met in the street?**

1st lesson:	
2nd lesson:	
	break
3rd lesson:	
4th lesson:	
	lunch
5th lesson:	
6th lesson:	

Worksheets   *ch. 3*

A. Find all the place names on the map on p. 54.

B. Fill in the missing words.

Rosso said, "Now you know that I _____ to you. I don't live in a _____; my grandfather and I live in a _____. He runs a _____. The other children don't like me because we are _____. And what about you? Why are you _____ on me? Please, leave me _____."

Julia answered, "I want to be your _____. I like you. I think I ran away because I was _____. I wasn't _____ to see you."

Rosso was not angry any more. "All right," he said, "let's _____ again. We can have _____, but no more _____. Can I come and _____ your parents now?"

"No," Julia replied, "it's not _____; my father is _____ _____ and my mother is very _____. Come tomorrow afternoon and _____ me with my English."

C. Can you explain this sentence?

> They were both alone, but in different ways. (p. 13, l. 4)

▷ _____
_____
_____
_____

Worksheets Ch. 4

A. Finish the sentences.

1. On Sunday Julia and Rosso _____

2. On Monday they decided _____

3. Shorty was interested in Rosso because _____

4. Rosso's grandfather said, "When I was a boy _____

B.

> Rosso said to Shorty, "Julia is not my girlfriend."
> – Was that a lie?

▷ _____

C. Take a pencil and draw Rosso's and Julia's route through the West End into your map of London on p. 54.

D. Find these sentences and phrases in the text and write them down.

1. Halte dich von Shorty fern. ▷ _____

2. Ich war gestern bei dir zu Hause. ▷ _____

3. Sie wollen, dass ich Mitglied in ihrer Bande werde. ▷ _____

4. sich mit jemandem anfreunden ▷ _____

5. Als ich in Rossos Alter war... ▷ _____

6. Ich habe gelernt, wie man Autos repariert. ▷ _____

E. Questions – questions – questions!
Mrs Miller, an English neighbour, was having tea with Julia's mother. The two women asked Julia a lot of questions when she came home on Monday. Write down Julia's answers.

1. How did you get to Oxford Circus? ▷ _____

2. What did you see in the West End? ▷ _____

3. Where does Rosso live? ▷ _____

4. Isn't everything very dirty there? ▷ _____

5. What do you like about this boy, Julia? ▷ _____

Worksheets ch. 5

A. Right or wrong? – Correct the wrong statements, please.

1. There is not much green in London, there are only dirty houses and grey streets. ▷ _____

2. Lots of boys and girls at the school are jealous of Julia's and Rosso's friendship. ▷ _____

3. Rosso was sad because in the Easter holidays he would not see Shorty Mulligan. ▷ _____

4. One evening Rosso took Julia to a little park on the north bank of the Thames. ▷ _____

5. Julia thought that the park was very romantic. ▷ _____

6. She gave Rosso a whistle as a present. ▷ _____

7. When a Romany hears the sound of the whistle, he or she knows that somebody is in danger. ▷ _____

8. Rosso had made the whistle himself. ▷ _____

9. Later they went all the way home hand in hand. ▷ _____

B. A tour of London
1. Can you find the names of 10 famous places and sights in London?

```
B U C K I N G H A M F P A L A C E S U P
I T T U O J Z T A H G I R E U I O K N F
G E E R T J K U U I O C A G D E N T O W
T T S T R P A U L ' S E C A T H E D R A L
B J O O C H R T U I H A G U U K L Y X C
E W E W E O H Z K Z U D I Y H B J W F K
N H J E G F E R U T H I F E D A E E S R
K O P R B O A P E H A L E M O T T S P A
M E R L O P T X P A R L I A M E N T O P
W O R H T A H H L M M Y B V C A R N O L
M U N E T B R G P E N C I P O I L E I A
M A D A M E O T U S S A U D ' S O N N I D
S Y H O O M W I G E F M O O V E R D A Y
H T E O X F O R D R S T R E E T O L A H
```

2. What would you like to see in London? – Why?

▷ _____
_____

_____
_____

_____
_____

_____
_____

Worksheets ch. 6

ROSSO

▶ **A. What happened? – Find the right sentences.**

1. On | Easter Sunday / Saturday afternoon / Sunday morning | two men / a woman / a man | wanted to talk to Rosso's | parents. / father. / grandfather.

2. After | polishing / repairing / driving | the car Rosso | locked | the caravan. / it. / the garage.

3. He went for a walk | with the dog. / with Julia. / on his own.

4. He bought | cigarettes / a newspaper / a chocolate bar | for Jake.

5. He was very | happy / surprised / angry | when he read about a gang of | three / four / six | men,

   who had | robbed a bank / stolen gold / killed a prison doctor | two / seven / fifteen | years ago.

6. One of the men was | Jake, Rosso's father / Raymond, Rosso's father / Jake, Rosso's grandfather | who lived in | France / Italy / Belgium | now.

7. Rosso was | very worried about / interested in / looking forward to | what | Shorty Mulligan / Julia / Gerry Smith | would think of his family.

8. When Rosso met Shorty, the two boys | had a friendly talk. / did not talk to each other. / began to fight.

12

B. Looking at the background.

1. Why is Rosso's father hiding from the police?
   ▷ _____
   _____
   _____
   _____

2. What happened to the other members of the gang?
   ▷ _____
   _____
   _____
   _____
   _____
   _____
   _____

3. Does Rosso think that his father is a criminal?
   ▷ _____
   _____
   _____

4. Why is the crime in the press again after such a long time?
   ▷ _____
   _____
   _____
   _____

Worksheets — Ch. 7

A. Complete the following sentences.

1. After Rosso had heard the telephone ring, his grandfather …
2. At one o'clock Rosso woke again because …
3. In the garage he saw … who were …
4. Suddenly one of the men …
5. In the fuse-box next to the garage Rosso …
6. When the men were in the yard, Rosso …
7. In the garage he found … and … the caravan.
8. Rosso was afraid because …
9. Suddenly he knew that …

B. A crime puzzle!
Find the right words. The letters in the shaded boxes will give you the name of a person or criminal who helps other criminals.

1. a person who breaks into people's houses
2. people who have to arrest criminals
3. Murder is a … .
4. Gerry Smith is a … .
5. Rosso switched on the … in the yard.
6. a place where criminals must stay for a long time
7. a slang term for what thieves have stolen
8. the opposite of 'innocent'
9. a person who does illegal things
10. It is the job of the police to … criminals.

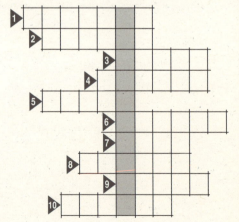

Worksheets

Ch. 8

A. Translation exercise
After the argument between Julia and her parents Mrs Witzkow told their neighbour, Mr Miller, about it. Below is the argument the Witzkows had.

> Mr Witzkow: „Deine Mutter und ich glauben nicht, dass du mit Rosso soviel Zeit verbringen solltest. Sein Vater ist ein Verbrecher."
>
> Julia: „Das ist nicht wahr! Und Rosso kennst du nicht. Er ist ein ganz normaler Mensch – genauso wie wir!"
>
> Mrs Witzkow: „Vielleicht solltest du dich mit ihm nicht so oft treffen."
>
> Julia: „Ich werde mich mit ihm so oft treffen, wie ich will. Ihr habt mich hierher gebracht, und jetzt, wo ich einen richtigen Freund gefunden habe, wollt ihr nicht, dass ich ihn sehe. Das ist einfach nicht fair."
>
> Mr Witzkow: „Jetzt gehst du in dein Zimmer und kommst erst wieder, wenn du dich entschuldigen willst."

Write down what Mrs Witzkow said.

"My husband and Julia have just had a terrible argument. He said to her, '____

____

____

Julia answered, '____

____

I suggested, '____

Then Julia shouted, '____

____

____

____

My husband replied, '____

____ "

ch. 9

A. Find the missing words.

1. The man who was waiting in front of the scrapyard was
   _____ .

2. He saw that Julia _____ over the wall.

3. Suddenly his _____ drove quickly out of the yard.

4. In it were _____ .

5. He _____ them, but after some time he stopped at a _____ .

6. He dialled _____ and told the _____ that Julia had been _____ .

7. Julia's parents met Rosso at _____ .

8. Mr Witzkow was very _____ and _____ and told a _____ that his daughter was missing.

B. Find words and expressions in the text that could substitute the words in italics.

1. One minute *passed.* ▷ _____

2. This number is only for *people in dangerous situations.* ▷ _____
   _____

3. Your people would like *to talk to me.* ▷ _____

4. It is *almost twelve o'clock in the night.* ▷ _____

5. *Nobody knows where our daughter Julia is.* ▷ _____
   _____

6. *The police will stop us because we are driving too fast.* ▷ _____
   _____

7. It *did not help.* ▷ _____

Worksheets *Ch. 10*

▶ **A. There are seven scenes in this chapter. Fill in the table.**

scene & place	action
1. p. 42, l. 1 – p. 43, l. 26 police station; in a police car	
2. p. ...	
3.	
4.	
5.	
6.	
7.	

Worksheets — Ch. 10

scenes 1 – 4

B. Right or wrong? – Correct the wrong statements.

1. The sergeant at the police station asked Julia's parents to stay there.
   ▷ _____
   _____

2. Rosso would recognize the old Riley anywhere. ▷ _____
   _____

3. It was lucky for Julia that she did not have the right key.
   ▷ _____
   _____

4. Ray found his father in the back of a car. ▷ _____
   _____

5. Jason helped Ray to free Julia. ▷ _____
   _____

C. Vocabulary. All the words are in the text. Can you find them?

1. a policeman who does not wear a uniform ▷ _____
   _____

2. it helps you to identify a car or a motorbike ▷ _____
   _____

3. a place where you can repair things ▷ _____

4. the part of a car which you can put bags and boxes in ▷ _____
   _____

5. a person who is kept prisoner by other people ▷ _____
   _____

scenes 5 – 7

D. Put the parts of the sentences together correctly.

1. When they were in Jamaica Road,	a) there was a service tunnel.
2. The policemen in the blue Ford Escort	b) because she knew some judo tricks.
3. Inspector Darrow was angry	c) Rosso suddenly saw the Riley.
4. In the middle of the tunnel	d) because he wanted to revenge himself on his cousin.
5. Gerry had hidden the loot	e) that they had lost the gangsters.
6. He used Ray's old car	f) they found the loot in some metal boxes.
7. Julia was able to escape	g) did not see the gangsters at their end of the tunnel.
8. After the police had arrested the criminals,	h) in the service tunnel seven years before.

E. The police need a plan of the area where the gangsters were arrested. Can you make one for them?

Worksheets — Ch. 11

A. Ray's story. Put the sentences in the right order.

- Two of Gerry's men tried to steal my old car but weren't able to.
- When I heard that Gerry had escaped from prison, I wanted him to lead me to where the bullion was hidden.
- After that I rescued my father.
- Somebody told Jake that his dog had been found.
- I followed them and phoned the police.
- Then I went to the tunnel in a police car.
- Afterwards I ran away for seven years.
- I told Rosso to send Julia to the caravan.
- The gangsters kidnapped him.
- Then I saw them driving away with Julia in my Riley.
- After the robbery I drove Gerry's car into the side of a bridge.

B. Working on the language
a) Use the right tenses: simple past – past perfect.

1. The gangsters _____ (not be able) to drive the Riley away, because Rosso _____ (take out) the rotor arm.

2. Rosso _____ (tell) Ray that Sid Mulligan _____ (see) Julia at the yard.

3. The police _____ (go) to the tunnel after they _____ (rescue) Rosso's grandfather.

4. Rosso _____ (want) to know why his father _____ (never write) in all those years.

b) **Put the sentences into the passive voice.**

1. The gangsters kidnapped Jake.

   ▷ _____

2. Gerry had hidden the loot in the tunnel.

   ▷ _____

   _____

3. The police arrested the criminals and found the bullion.

   ▷ _____

   _____

4. Maybe the insurance company will give Ray a small reward.

   ▷ _____

   _____

C. **In some words the letters have got mixed up. Correct the mistakes.**

1. Ray wanted to catch the gang edr-dehdna ▷ _____

2. He had had to live without his family. That had been his untnimepsh.

   ▷ _____

3. The whole story had been a big dvaenteur for Jason, too.

   ▷ _____

D. **A few final tasks**

1. Imagine you are a reporter and have to write about the police action in the tunnel. Using quotes from the characters write a short report for your newspaper.
2. Write down three questions you would like to ask either Rosso or Julia. Your partner imagines that he or she is Rosso or Julia and has to answer your questions.
3. Julia had been in great danger. Do you think Ray was right to send her to the yard? He said, 'That was a risk I had to take.' Do you agree?

Worksheets — Ch. 1

The Australian Connection

○ **A. Answer the questions.**

1. What had Alex been waiting for for eight weeks? ▷ _____
   _____

2. What had his mother promised him? ▷ _____
   _____

3. How long is it since he last saw his father? ▷ _____
   _____

4. Where does he want to travel to? ▷ _____
   _____

5. What does his mother think about that? ▷ _____
   _____

6. What did Alex write in the letter to his father? ▷ _____
   _____

7. What did he do to earn money for the trip? ▷ _____
   _____

8. What did Tom send with his letter? ▷ _____
   _____

9. What were Alex's feelings when he got the letter from his father?
   ▷ _____
   _____

Worksheets Ch. 2

A. Suddenly Alex had two families. Fill in the names below:

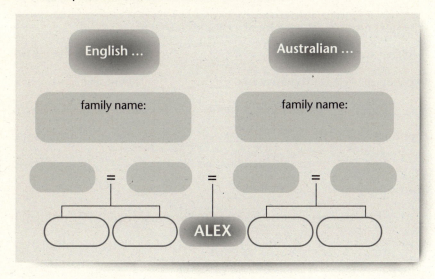

B. Answer the questions.
1. At London airport Alex had mixed feelings. Why?
2. What did Mary tell him about his father?
3. Why was Alex angry?
4. Where did they all go after Alex had had breakfast?
5. What do you learn about Dani?
6. What did Alex do on his first evening in Sydney? And on his second?

C. What a mess! The letters in some of the words have got mixed up in these sentences. Correct the mixed-up words.
1. At the airport Alex felt very nfcoedus. ▷ _____
2. After saying goodbye he went to the turedepar nlogue.
   ▷ _____
3. When Alex heard that Dani was in a pop group, he was very imspdrese. ▷ _____

Worksheets   Ch. 3

A. In this summary some words are missing. Put in suitable words.

The next morning Mary told Alex that his father _____ back before the 17th. She _____ that Alex should visit her brother in Adelaide and meet her _____ Kevin. Everything was _____ and Alex went to Adelaide by coach. On the way he got an impression of the _____ of the continent. In Adelaide he _____ by Kevin. The two boys liked _____ from the beginning.

The next day Kevin and Alex went to Kangaroo Island. Alex thought it was _____ there. He especially liked all the wild animals which were not _____ of people. At the campfire he wrote a _____ to his parents in England. The boys stayed there for _____ days.

After a short stop in Adelaide they left for Wilpena Pound. As they drove north, the land became _____ and _____, as they travelled into the "_____". They saw _____ towns and _____ with Aboriginal paintings. They left early the next day to climb one of the highest _____. This took them four hours. From the top they had a fantastic _____, but on the way down they got _____ to the skin from a heavy downpour.

Alex was very angry with his father, because he had learnt from Kevin that Tom hadn't told Kevin that he had been _____ in England and had a _____ there. He was so annoyed that he did not _____ any more if he saw Tom in Sydney or not. But finally he did take the coach back to Sydney.

Worksheets   Ch. 4

A. Finish the sentences.

1. Back in Sydney, Alex was very nervous because he thought _____.

2. Mary told him that Tom _____.

3. Dani invited him to _____.

4. In Melbourne Alex and the Beat Crew _____.

5. On the beach Alex and Dani _____.

6. Later they had a disagreement because _____.

7. Alex said that Tom and he could _____.

B. Find the right words from the text.

1. more than smiling ▷ _____
2. a light rain ▷ _____
3. to drive very fast ▷ _____
4. to move your head to say yes ▷ _____
5. at a concert the artists stand on a … ▷ _____
6. when you have a lot to do you have a … ▷ _____
7. cream that protects skin from getting burnt ▷ _____
8. ice-cream … in the sun ▷ _____

Worksheets

Ch. 4

▶ **C.** Now you have to find definitions for the following words from the text.

1. plenty of time ▷ _____
   _____

2. spotlight ▷ _____
   _____

3. to get lost ▷ _____
   _____

4. reception ▷ _____
   _____

5. to be busy ▷ _____
   _____

6. familiar ▷ _____
   _____

▶ **D.** What are the following instruments called in English?

✱ **E.** Imagine you are Alex. Write about your experiences in your diary again. Write about Australia, the Beat Crew, Dani and Tom.

✱ **F.** Design a poster for one of your gigs in Melbourne. Even if you are not good at drawing, make a rough sketch showing what elements you would like to include. What text would you use to encourage people to come and see your gig?

Worksheets Ch. 5

A. These statements are all incorrect. Change them so that they become correct.

1. The journey back to Sydney was without any problems.

    ▷ _____

    _____

2. The woman who helped them was Japanese.

    ▷ _____

    _____

3. They stopped in the Blue Mountains to look at the view.

    ▷ _____

    _____

4. While he was waiting for Terry to come back, Alex wrote another letter to his parents.

    ▷ _____

    _____

5. The mechanic wanted three hundred dollars for some very difficult repairs on the car.

    ▷ _____

    _____

6. When Alex saw Mary in the audience he got shaky fingers.

    ▷ _____

    _____

B. Draw a circle round the 'odd man out'.

1. car – van – bike – lorry

2. spare tyre – puncture – wheel – boot

3. get held up – be delayed – late – on time

4. painter – audience – gig – stage

Worksheets — **Ch. 6**

A. Right or Wrong? – Correct the wrong statements.

1. Tom took Alex in his arms. ▷

2. Tom and Alex made a lot of jokes. ▷

3. Alex was afraid of starting to cry. ▷

4. Tom knew Alex's birthday, he hadn't forgotten it. ▷

5. Alex decided to go on a trip with Dani. ▷

6. Dani took Alex upstairs into her room. ▷

7. During the trip with his father Alex slept most of the time.
   ▷

8. Once they had to stop because there was so much mud on the road.
   ▷

9. The next couple of days were very exciting for Alex. ▷

10. He was very happy that he had found his father at last. ▷

B. Find the right words. The letters in the shaded boxes will give you the name of a beautiful insect.

1. the instrument that Alex plays → ■ □ □ □   □ □ □ □ □ □
2. the people who listen to a concert → □ ■ □ □ □ □ □ □
3. when you have only got a mother → □ □ ■ □ □ □ □ □ □ □
4. area where there are lots of trees → □ □ □ □ □ ■
5. Alex took one to Sydney → □ □ □ □ ■
6. an Australian animal → □ □ □ □ □ ■ □ □
7. when musicians are on a stage → □ □ □ ■ □ □ □ □ □ □
8. another word for disagreement → □ □ □ □ ■ □ □ □
9. Alex writes everything into it → □ □ □ □ ■

C. How many words dealing with nature can you find?

S	U	G	A	R	X	C	A	N	E	A	M
W	R	T	P	K	O	U	R	C	O	P	H
A	H	U	W	L	R	R	O	N	E	L	I
M	U	D	D	Y	A	E	M	R	O	I	N
P	A	U	T	F	N	N	K	I	K	A	S
L	I	G	E	H	L	O	T	V	J	N	E
L	B	E	A	C	H	L	Y	E	Y	A	C
A	R	A	I	N	X	F	O	R	E	S	T

29

Worksheets — Ch. 7

A. Sentence building.
Use these words to make complex sentences:

> when – after – because – although – which – who – and – until – as

1. The sun was rising.
   Tom steered out of the harbour.

2. Gypsy Woman was a sailing boat.
   It was 9 metres long.

3. They had breakfast.
   Then Alex lay back on the deck.

4. Alex was diving.
   He saw beautiful fish.
   He thought it was fantastic.

5. The sun was too hot.
   Tom told Alex to come out of the water.

6. He went swimming and diving again in the afternoon.
   He felt very happy.
   He saw what he thought was a shark.

7. Alex was shouting for help.
   Tom only laughed.
   It was not a dangerous animal.

8. Alex had not been in real danger.
   He hated Tom for laughing at him.

9. On Whitsunday Island it rained heavily.
   It made everything wet – sleeping bags, towels, clothes.
   It washed away all their cooking utensils.

10. Alex asked Tom why he had left his family in England.
    Tom told that he had been afraid of settling down and becoming an adult.

11. Alex wrote in his diary again.
    He understood what Tom meant very well.

B. What is your opinion?
Do you think Tom was right to leave his wife and son all those years ago? Give reasons for your answer.

Worksheets

Ch. 8

✱ **A. These sentences are in the wrong order. Find the correct one.**

- Their manager arranged a tour all over the country.
- After a shower he went to the TV studio.
- One day, after a long time, Alex and Dani were enjoying a free afternoon together at Byron Bay.
- The highway back to Sydney was noisy and crowded.
- Dani told him that they were at number one in the hit list.
- Alex and his father spent the time swimming, snorkelling, fishing and lying in the sun.
- And Alex became a well-known person who was interviewed and who appeared in talk-shows.
- They were his favourite animals.
- Mary told Alex that the band was expecting him the same evening.
- On Whitsunday Island it was peaceful and quiet.
- Alex thought that his life was magical, like a fairy-tale.
- Finally they arrived in Sydney.
- From the lighthouse Dani showed him a group of dolphins in the water.
- The group became a really big success.
- He realized that the dolphins were different because they were free.

✱ **B. A reporter from an Australian youth magazine interviewed Alex. He asked him about his family, why he was in Australia, his interests, friends, career, etc. Write this interview.**

Worksheets — Ch. 9

A. Why did the career of the Beat Crew come to an end?
Make a list of some of the reasons.

▷ _____

_____

_____

_____

_____

_____

B. Alex felt he was in a dilemma. Why?

On the one hand …

On the other hand …

C. You are Alex. You are sitting in a small hotel room and writing in your diary. Write about your thoughts and feelings. Decide what you want to do in the future.

Worksheets — Ch. 10

A. Some important things happened which are not told in the book before the chapter begins. Make a list of these things.

- _____
- _____
- _____
- _____
- _____
- _____
- _____
- _____

B. Why did Dani and Alex call their band 'The Dolphins'?

C. In the book there are a lot of words about

▶ Family ▶ Nature ▶ The Sea ▶ Traffic ▶ Show Business

Work together in groups and make mind-maps.

D. Ideas for creative writing

1. In his diary Alex wrote that he had talked to Tom about the decisions he had to make and about Tom's reaction.
Write this dialogue.

2. Alex is back in London with his mother. She wants to know about his feelings towards Tom and Dani, his experiences in Australia, etc.
Write down some questions his mother might ask him and write down Alex's answers.

3. Alex writes a letter to his grandmother (his mother's mother) in Scotland. He tells her about everything that happened to him. Write the letter, including not only the facts but also his thoughts and feelings.

Worksheets — Ch. 1

A. What do we learn about Thomas's new school? Fill in a few keywords.

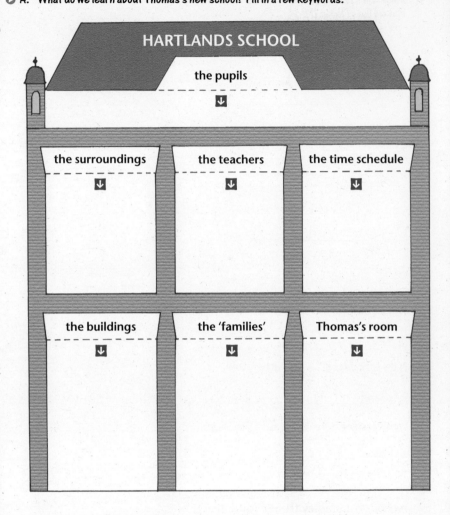

B. Answer the following questions:

1. What are we told about Thomas's parents?
2. Do you like his mother? Why, or why not?
3. Would you like to go to school at Hartlands? Give reasons for your answer.

C. Imagine you are Thomas. Write a diary entry for your first day at school.

Worksheets Ch. 2

A. Finish the sentences.

1. At 10 o'clock John Clay heard … ▷ _____
   _____
   _____
   _____

2. When he heard a military voice and a whistle, he wanted …
   ▷ _____
   _____

3. At 11 o'clock Mrs Winterton asked him … ▷ _____
   _____
   _____

4. When Clay went into the room, he found… ▷ _____
   _____
   _____

5. The pupils only left the room when … ▷ _____
   _____
   _____

6. Miller told Clay that … ▷ _____
   _____

7. Miller told Bradley that … ▷ _____
   _____

B. On his first night at Hartlands Thomas got 'the treatment'.
What happened to him? Do you think it was funny?

C. Imagine you are Ralph, Thomas's room-mate.
Write a letter to your parents in which you talk about yourself and your new room-mate.

35

Worksheets Ch. 2

D. Find the right words from the text.

1. a large room where you do sports

   ▷ _____

2. a room at a boarding school where the pupils sleep

   ▷ _____

3. You can put your clothes in it.

   ▷ _____

4. You can't open the door because you have no key. The door is…

   ▷ _____

5. If something which another person does disturbs or annoys you, you go to that person and … about it.

   ▷ _____

6. If the TV is too loud you can …

   ▷ _____

7. When somebody has got something that you would like to have, you … that person.

   ▷ _____

8. You use it to dry your body.

   ▷ _____

E. So far we have met six important characters in the story:

▶ Thomas ▶ his mother ▶ Ralph ▶ Bradley ▶ Mr Clay
▶ Mr Miller

How will the story go on? Make some suggestions, mentioning each of the above.

Worksheets   Ch. 3

A. Answer the following questions:

1. What is the normal routine in the dining-room?

2. What behaviour does Mr Graham, the headmaster, expect from his pupils?

3. What does Mr Hansen think of Bradley?

B. Here are some answers. You have to find the questions.

1. ...? _____

   _____

   – Mr Graham spoke loudly and clearly.

2. ...? _____

   _____

   – He felt sorry for him.

3. ...? _____

   _____

   – He grinned openly.

4. ...? _____

   _____

   – He had been at Hartlands for almost two years.

5. ...? _____

   _____

   – Because nobody could prove anything

6. ...? _____

   _____

   – They asked him to play rugby with them.

Worksheets — Ch. 4

Betrayed

A. Here are some words and expressions. You have to decide if they can be used to describe Bradley or not.
Write the words in the table below.

> bossy   cheerful   helpful   polite   a good friend
> friendly   impertinent   threatening   respectful   shy
> nervous   frightened   intimidating   thoughtful
> honest   a bully   self-confident   fair   gentle
> loud   rude   cowardly   arrogant   timid   strong

⬇
BRADLEY
⬇

Yes	No

Worksheets — ch. 5

A. Read the beginning of chapter 4 again and make an advertisement for the pub in the Hartlands school magazine. The one below might help you, but you can design your own if you wish:

Come to our school pub!!!

Open every evening

from _____ till _____

Here you can _____

_____

_____ .

The atmosphere is _____ .

You can have a great evening at the Hartlands Pub.

You don't have to _____

to enjoy yourself.

The Pub Team

B. Answer the following questions.

1. Not everyone is happy about the way Bradley organizes the pub. Why not?

2. What kind of person is Bradley's father? Think of his social status and his behaviour in Mr Richards's office.

3. Why had he come to see Mr Richards in the first place?

4. Make a list of the things he mentioned to Mr Richards. Would you say that his visit was successful?

C. In the evening Mr Richards went home and talked to his wife about Mr Bradley's visit. Write the dialogue. You can start like this:

Mr Richards: Guess who came into my office today. I was just answering a phone call when …

Worksheets — Ch. 6

**A. Here is a sketch of the drama room.
Write the words and names in the right places.**

> the audience   Mr Hansen   cheered   clapped   Bradley
> the prosecutor   Mr Graham   the jury   the hero
> the defendant   the judge   banged their feet   whistled
> exchanged arguments

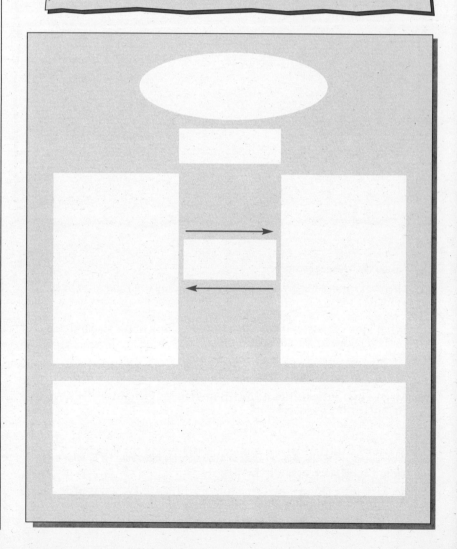

B. Make lists of Mr Hansen's and Bradley's arguments.

Mr Hansen's arguments:

▷ _____

Bradley's arguments:

▷ _____

C. What do you think?

1. Whose arguments do you find more convincing?

2. What was Mr Graham's judgment at the end of the inquiry?

3. Have you any idea where Bradley's documents might have come from so suddenly?

4. Do you think that such a public inquiry is a good idea?

Worksheets — Ch. 7

Betrayed

⊗ **A. Paragraph writing.**
Use the words on the right to connect the sentences on the left. Watch out for the tenses!

1. One afternoon John Clay (*walk*) to the ruin. It (*be*) on the top of one of the hills near the school.	*which*
2. He (*arrive*). He (*think*) he was alone. He (*be*) not.	*when* *but*
3. Mr Clay (*realize*) that it (*be*) Thomas Walker. He (*go*) over to him. He (*find*) it difficult to start a conversation. It (*be*) not a normal school situation.	*after* *but* *because*
4. Mr Clay (*apologize*). He (*not have*) enough time for the quieter pupils.	*for* (+gerund)
5. He (*realize*). There (*be*) a secret world in the dormitories. It (*be*) hidden from the teachers and (*be*) full of violence and power.	*that* *which*
6. They (*walk*) back to the school grounds. They (*see*) Bradley. He (*sit*) in a large car.	*when* *who*
7. Mr Clay (*be*) very friendly to the boy. Thomas (*not want*) to say anything about Bradley.	*although*
8. In the office a policeman (*inform*) Mr Clay. They (*catch*) a pupil. He (*ride*) too fast on a motorbike and (*not have*) any papers. That (*be*) a serious offence.	*that* *who* *who* *which*

Start like this:

1. One afternoon John Clay walked to the ruin which was ...

B. What do you think? Write down a paragraph giving your opinion of each of the following statements.

1.
> "..it's always the pupils who cause problems who get the attention. You easily forget the others." (p. 48, ll. 27-28)

– Do you agree?

2.
> "He knew also that there was a world of violence and power in those rooms, a secret world that was hidden from him and that disappeared as soon as he arrived." (p. 48, l. 35 – p. 49, l. 3)

– Is it like that at your school, too?

3.
> "I'm sorry, Mr Clay. I'm not an informer." (p. 50, l. 19)

– Do you think it is right not to tell teachers when there is a problem among the pupils?

C. What's that in English? Find the expressions in the text.

1. Er atmete schwer. ▷ _____

2. Die Zeit vergeht so schnell. ▷ _____

3. Thomas zuckte mit den Schultern. ▷ _____
   _____

4. Ich könnte vielleicht bei ihr in der Schweiz leben. ▷ _____
   _____

Worksheets — Ch. 8

Betrayed

▶ **A.** Right (R) or wrong (W)? Or 'not in the text' (N)? Put in the appropriate letter in the box and correct the statement if it is wrong.

1. Bradley was quite nervous when he came to John Clay's room. ☐ _____

2. He was very sorry for having sold a motorbike to Peters. ☐ _____

3. The bike was properly taxed and insured. ☐ _____

4. Bradley said that Clay could use Peters as an informer. ☐ _____

5. Bradley's friends beat Thomas up because Bradley had sent them. ☐ _____

6. Everybody could see that Thomas was fighting with the boys and needed help. ☐ _____

7. Thomas became an informer. ☐ _____

✶ **B.** Imagine you are Thomas. Before going to bed you write a few lines in your diary. You could start like this:

> *It is terrible here, and it is getting worse every day.*
> *This afternoon ...*

C. Match these words to the characters:

> a bit nervous   frightened   inconsiderate   violent
> self-confident   hurt   serious, but not too strict
> a gang   a victim   isolated   kind
> a good athlete   helpful   cowardly   cruel

Thomas	John Clay	Bradley	Bradley's friends

D. Match the first and second parts of these expressions:

1. to run
2. to listen
3. to feel
4. to be crazy
5. to have
6. to pick up
7. to shout for
8. to keep
9. to take
10. to make

a) a seat
b) a hot shower
c) a ball
d) help
e) your mouth shut
f) a pub
g) a circle
h) about bikes
i) carefully
j) helpless

Worksheets — Ch. 9

A. Find the right words to complete the sentences.

1. After Thomas had left him, Mr Clay went to ▷ _____.

   a) the headmaster
   b) the secretary
   c) Mr Hansen
   d) the school trustees

2. The problem of the school was that they were losing ▷ _____.

   a) pupils
   b) expenses
   c) teachers
   d) figures

3. Some parents were complaining about ▷ _____.

   a) too much discipline
   b) too little freedom
   c) not enough discipline
   d) too much freedom and discipline

4. To improve the financial situation the chairman suggested ▷ _____
   _____.

   a) returning to stricter methods
   b) dismissing some of the people who worked at the school
   c) sending some of the pupils home
   d) hiring new teachers

B. Talking about the text

1. What is Mr Graham's idea of a good school? Do all the parents agree with him?
2. 'Last hired, first fired' – what does that mean?
3. Explain in your own words why Mr Graham is in a difficult position.
4. What question is still open at the end of the chapter?

C. In the text below, the prepositions have been left out. Fill them in.

The school trustees met _____ the headmaster's office because they were worried _____ the financial situation _____ the school. The school had been losing some _____ its pupils and there wasn't a long waiting list _____ parents who wanted to send their children _____ the school. Although there were some letters _____ worried parents, Mr Graham believed the majority _____ parents were happy _____ the way the school was run and felt that their children were _____ good hands.

However, the trustees, while not wanting to return _____ stricter methods, wanted to see some changes. After studying the costs _____ all sides, they had come _____ the conclusion that the headmaster should reduce the number _____ people employed _____ the school.

Mr Graham was shocked _____ the suggestion. He looked down _____ the papers _____ the table and felt that everything had been reduced _____ numbers, that everything was seen _____ the form _____ profit or loss.

He breathed _____ deeply and pushed his chair back _____ the table and suggested that they take a break.

Later he would have to look _____ the contracts and then decide who he should fire.

Worksheets — ch. 10

Betrayed

✲ A. Finish the sentences.

1. When they were sitting on the bench Mr Clay did not listen to Mr Hansen's words because …

2. All the lights in the boys' rooms went out except for …

3. Clay said that Mr Graham had … and that he had not …

4. At quarter to eight …

5. Hansen and Clay walked along the dark corridor and …

6. They could hear …

7. Hansen banged … and shouted …

8. Bradley and Dexter had broken the school rules because …

9. The large white thing in the corner that Hansen saw …

10. Suddenly the two teachers heard Jackie who …

11. Bradley took a plastic bag …

12. The teachers were not able …

13. Bradley and his friends …

> In the end Mr Clay hit Bradley.
> What do you think of that?

✲ B. What's that in German?

1. as far as I know (p. 63, l. 27)

2. Any idea what it's about? (p. 64, l. 6)

3. That's where you are wrong (p. 67, l. 3)

4. I couldn't help it (p. 69, ll. 1f.)

Worksheets — Ch. 11

A. Mr Graham, the headmaster, and Mr Hansen had a serious discussion about what to do with Bradley. – Make a list of their arguments.

Mr Graham

▷

Mr Hansen

▷

And you? – What is your opinion? Whose arguments do you find stronger?

Worksheets

Ch. 11

B. A puzzle. (You can find all the words on pages 71–73.)

1. The boys are not allowed to drink it.
2. referring to money
3. not to let sb. finish a sentence
4. the opinion that people have about another person
5. to make a pupil leave a school and not come back
6. a room with lots of books
7. The clock strikes twelve, but it is not noon.
8. a task or action that you have to perform
9. to talk about a thing, giving one's opinions and views on it

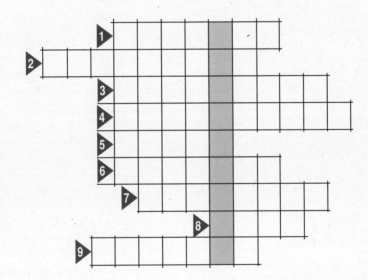

C. Discuss the following in class.

1. Do you think Mr Graham did do a deal with Bradley's father?
2. What would you have done if you had been the headmaster?
3. Why did Mr Hansen and Mr Clay have to leave the school?

D. Some language work: Imagine you are a teacher who was at the meeting and you have to tell another colleague who missed it what was said. – Put the following dialogue into indirect speech. Try to make it sound fluid, i.e. do not change it word for word.

'What Bradley did was a serious crime,' said Hansen. 'Hand him over to the police. He belongs in prison. That's the only place where he will realize how many mistakes he has made.'

'I needn't remind you, Mr Hansen,' said the headmaster 'that you have no proof. We only have Bradley's words. He confessed and told us what he knew – if he could have one last chance.'

'In other words he has done a deal with you. We are covering up,' said Mr Hansen. 'We are letting him walk away free.' (p. 73)

Worksheets — Ch. 11

Betrayed

▶ **E. If-clauses. Finish Mr Graham's sentences:**

1. If we (*keep*) _____ Bradley at our school, _____
   _____

2. If he (*fail*) _____ his A-levels at the end of the year,
   _____

3. If we (*keep*) _____ all the teachers here, _____
   _____

4. If the press (*find*) _____ out about the drugs, _____
   _____

5. If you (*give*) _____ me any concrete proof of Bradley's drug dealing, _____
   _____

REMEMBER:
If-clause – simple present
main clause – will-future or auxiliaries

✱ **F. Ideas for creative writing.**

1. Mr Graham said that he had talked to Bradley's father on the phone (pp. 72–73). Write down the dialogue between the two men.

2. One of the teachers in the school library had to write a record of the teachers' meeting. Write this text, using indirect speech.

3. After the teachers' meeting Mr Hansen and Mr Clay went to Mr Clay's room. They were shocked and angry and talked to each other for a long time. Write a dialogue of their talk.

Worksheets — Ch. 12

A. More questions!

1. Why did Bradley go to Thomas's room?

2. What do you think were the author's intentions when writing this chapter?

3. Do you like the ending of the story? Why (not)?
   The following words may help you:

   → just – unjust – realistic – sad – normal – happy ending – boring – interesting

B. Looking at the language.

Find expressions from the text which say that somebody is shocked and frightened. (Look at chapter 11, too.)

_____

_____

_____

C. Think about what might happen next and continue the chapter.

D. Make a mind-map of all the 'school' words you know. You can choose different ways to arrange the words. Look at this example:

solutions to the worksheets — Ch. 1

A.

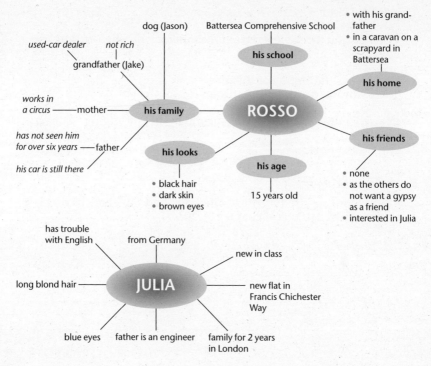

B.

1. ▷ He is a gypsy. He lives with his grandfather in a caravan and has no brothers or sisters; the others live with their parents in houses.
2. ▷ The other children don't like gypsies. They think they are lazy. They do not want to sit next to him in class, or play with him.
3. ▷ She wants him to go school and have a better chance in life. As she travels a lot, it would be difficult for Rosso to go to school.
4. ▷ Jake does not talk about Rosso's father, but thinks he will come back one day, so he keeps his car ready for him.
5. ▷ Jake wants him to find a good job, so he can get regular wages, paid holidays and a pension when he stops working.
6. ▷ Rosso wanted to keep a diary so he could write about Julia.
7. ▷ Julia is a new girl in his class. She is from Angermünde in Germany.

C.

1. ▷ caravan
2. ▷ lonely
3. ▷ scrapyard
4. ▷ wages
5. ▷ garage

solutions to the worksheets — Ch. 2

A.

1. ▷ She had just made new friends in Hechingen and she hardly spoke any English.
2. ▷ Most of the houses are small, old and dirty. A lot of blacks and Asians live there.
3. ▷ She liked his dark eyes, his long black hair and the fact that he talked about interesting things.
4. ▷ She wanted to meet Rosso and perhaps see where he lived.
5. ▷ He was angry and unfriendly. At school he avoided her and hardly talked to her.
6. ▷ He had lied to her about his family and home and did not want her to find out the truth.

B.

1st lesson:	English
2nd lesson:	maths
	break
3rd lesson:	history
4th lesson:	French
	lunch
5th lesson:	PE (physical education)
6th lesson:	handicrafts

solutions to the worksheets — Ch. 3

A. – –

B.

Rosso said, "Now you know that I lied to you. I don't live in a house; my grandfather and I live in a caravan. He runs a scrapyard. The other children don't like me because we are gypsies. And what about you? Why are you spying on me? Please, leave me alone."

Julia answered, "I want to be your friend. I like you. I think I ran away because I was frightened. I wasn't expecting to see you."

Rosso was not angry any more. "All right," he said, "let's start again. We can have secrets, but no more lies. Can I come and meet your parents now?"

"No," Julia replied, "it's not convenient; my father is at work and my mother is very busy. Come tomorrow afternoon and help me with my English."

C.

Neither of them has any friends and they are therefore lonely. Rosso, because he is a gypsy and the others do not want to be with him (prejudice); Julia, because she is new in England and her English is not very good. They are both outsiders.

solutions to the worksheets — ch. 4

A.
1. … went for a walk in Battersea Park and talked about the differences between Germany and Britain.
2. … to go and see the West End after school.
3. … he wanted him to join his gang. Rosso could be useful as he was able to drive a car.
4. … we moved around the country and only went to school in the winter for a few months every year.

B.

Up to now Rosso and Julia have only been friends. 'Girlfriend' implies romantic feelings.

C. – –

D.
1. ▷ Stay away from Shorty. (p. 15, l. 2)
2. ▷ I was at your place yesterday. (p. 16, ll. 8–9)
3. ▷ They want me to join their gang. (p. 17, l. 12)
4. ▷ make friends with somebody (p. 17, l. 27)
5. ▷ When I was Rosso's age … (p. 18, l. 6)
6. ▷ I learnt how to repair cars. (p. 18, l. 12)

E.
1. ▷ We took the number 19 bus.
2. ▷ We saw Oxford Street with its big shops and stores, Marble Arch, Park Lane, Hyde Park Corner, Piccadilly Circus with the statue of Eros.
3. ▷ He lives in a caravan with his grandfather.
4. ▷ I haven't been inside, so I don't know, but I think it's clean.
5. ▷ I like the way he looks and I like talking to him. He is interesting.

solutions to the worksheets — ch. 5

A.
1. ▷ Wrong. There are a lot of green parks in London.
2. ▷ Wrong. They smiled when they saw them together. Only Shorty was jealous.
3. ▷ Wrong. Rosso was glad that he would not see Shorty.
4. ▷ Right.
5. ▷ Wrong. She thought that life on a houseboat was romantic.
6. ▷ Wrong. Rosso gave her the whistle as a present.
7. ▷ Right.
8. ▷ Wrong. His mother gave it to him.
9. ▷ Right.

▶ B. 1.

```
B U C K I N G H A M F P A L A C E S U P
I T T U O J Z T A H G I R E U I O K N F
G E E R T J K U U I O C A G D E N T O W
T T S T R P A U L'S E C A T H E D R A L
B J O O C H R T U I H A G U U K L Y X C
E W E W E O H Z K Z U D I Y H B W F K
N H J E G F E R U T H I F E D A E E S R
K O P R B O A P E H A L E M O T T S P A
M E R L O P T X P A R L I A M E N T O P
W O R H T A H H L M M Y B V C A R N O L
M U N E T B R G P E N C I P O I L E I A
M A D A M E O T U S S A U D'S O N N I D
S Y H O O M W I G E F M O O V E R D A Y
H T E O X F O R D R S T R E E T O L A H
```

2. – –

solutions to the worksheets   ch. 6

▶ A.

1. On | Saturday afternoon | a man | wanted to talk to Rosso's | father.
2. After | polishing | the car Rosso | locked | it.
3. He went for a walk | on his own.
4. He bought | a newspaper | for Jake.
5. He was very | surprised | when he read about a gang of | four | men, | who had | stolen gold | seven | years ago.
6. One of the men was | Raymond, Rosso's father | who lived in | France | now.
7. Rosso was | very worried about | what | Julia | would think of his family.
8. When Rosso met Shorty, the two boys | began to fight.

▶ B.
1. ▷ The police thought that he had taken part in the bullion robbery seven years ago.
2. ▷ Sidney Mulligan and Albert Johnson came out of prison last year. Gerry Smith, the leader of the gang, was sent to prison for 15 years but escaped yesterday.
3. ▷ Rosso is convinced that his father is innocent.
4. ▷ Gerry Smith has just escaped from prison and half the bullion is still missing.

solutions to the worksheets — ch. 7

A.

1. ... drove away in the van.
2. ... he heard quiet noises in the yard.
3. ... two men ... searching through the old car.
4. ... found something in the car door.
5. ... pulled the master switch and the light went out in the garage.
6. ... turned on the burglar alarm.
7. ... a key ... took it to ...
8. ... Jake and Jason were not there.
9. ... he was not alone. A tall man was standing outside the garage door.

B.

1. BURGLAR
2. POLICE
3. CRIME
4. ROBBER
5. ALARM
6. PRISON
7. LOOT
8. GUILTY
9. CROOK
10. ARREST

solutions to the worksheets — ch. 8

A.

My husband and Julia have just had a terrible argument. He said to her, 'Your mother and I don't think that you should spend so much time with Rosso. His father's a criminal.'
Julia answered, 'That's not true. You don't even know Rosso. He's a normal person – just like us.'
I suggested, 'Perhaps you shouldn't meet him so often.'
Then Julia shouted, 'I'll meet him as often as I want to. You brought me here and now that I have a real friend, you don't want me to see him. That's just not fair.'
My husband replied, 'Go to your room right now and don't come out until you want to say you're sorry / to apologize.'

solutions to the worksheets — Ch. 9

A.

1. Raymond Smith, Rosso's father
2. was climbing
3. old Riley
4. Gerry Smith, Sid Mulligan and Julia
5. followed; phone box
6. 999; police; kidnapped
7. Piccadilly Circus
8. angry; worried; policeman

B.

1. ▷ went by (p. 38, l. 20)
2. ▷ emergencies (p. 39, l. 16)
3. ▷ to have a word with me (p. 39, l. 27)
4. ▷ nearly midnight (p. 40, l. 15)
5. ▷ Our daughter Julia is missing (p. 40, l. 20)
6. ▷ We'll be stopped for speeding (p. 40, l. 27)
7. ▷ was no good (p. 41, l. 5)

solutions to the worksheets — Ch. 10

A.

	scene & place	action
1.	p. 42, l. 1 – p. 43, l. 26 police station; in a police car	Rosso told the police about his father and his plan to catch the bullion thieves. Inspector Darrow said that the gangsters had Julia. They all drove off to find the Riley.
2.	p. 43, l. 27 – p. 44, l. 22 near the railway arches	Ray found the stolen Riley, freed Jason from the car boot and phoned the police again.
3.	p. 44, l. 23 – p. 45, l. 4 in the police car	Inspector Darrow was informed that the car had been found and that Julia and Jake were in Enid Street with the gang members.
4.	p. 45, l. 5 – p. 46, l. 3 at Arch Number Two, Enid St	After the gangsters had driven off with Julia, Ray freed Jake.
5.	p. 46, l. 4 – p. 47, l. 22 in the police car	The police followed the Riley to the Rothehithe Tunnel but then they lost it in the tunnel.
6.	p. 47, l. 23 – p. 48, l. 32 in the tunnel	The gangsters drove to the service tunnel where Gerry had hidden the loot. Julia managed to escape.
7.	p. 48, l. 33 – p. 50, l. 18 in the tunnel	Rosso heard Julia's whistle and ran towards her. Police cars moved down both ends. The gangsters were arrested and the loot was found in four metal boxes.

▶ **B.**
1. ▷ Wrong. The sergeant asked Julia's parents to go home.
2. ▷ Right.
3. ▷ Wrong. It was very dangerous for her that she had the wrong key.
4. ▷ Wrong. Ray found his father's dog in the boot of the car.
5. ▷ Wrong. Jason helped Ray to free Jake.

▶ **C.**
1. ▷ a plain-clothes policeman
2. ▷ a registration number
3. ▷ a workshop
4. ▷ a boot
5. ▷ a hostage

▶ **D.**

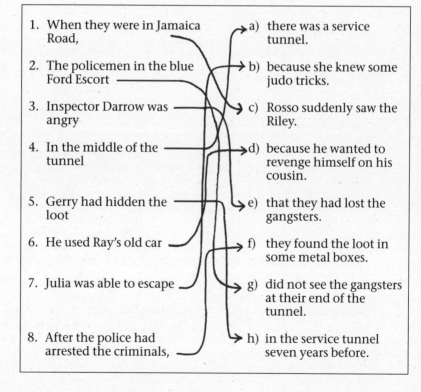

1. When they were in Jamaica Road,
2. The policemen in the blue Ford Escort
3. Inspector Darrow was angry
4. In the middle of the tunnel
5. Gerry had hidden the loot
6. He used Ray's old car
7. Julia was able to escape
8. After the police had arrested the criminals,

a) there was a service tunnel.
b) because she knew some judo tricks.
c) Rosso suddenly saw the Riley.
d) because he wanted to revenge himself on his cousin.
e) that they had lost the gangsters.
f) they found the loot in some metal boxes.
g) did not see the gangsters at their end of the tunnel.
h) in the service tunnel seven years before.

▶ **E.** --

solutions to the worksheets — Ch. 11

A.
- After the robbery I drove Gerry's car into the side of a bridge.
- Afterwards I ran away for seven years.
- When I heard that Gerry had escaped from prison, I wanted him to lead me to where the bullion was hidden.
- Somebody told Jake that his dog had been found.
- The gangsters kidnapped him.
- Two of Gerry's men tried to steal my old car but weren't able to.
- I told Rosso to send Julia to the caravan.
- Then I saw them driving away with Julia in my Riley.
- I followed them and phoned the police.
- After that I rescued my father.
- Then I went to the tunnel in a police car.

B.
a)
1. ▷ were not able; had taken out
2. ▷ told; had seen
3. ▷ went; had rescued
4. ▷ wanted; had never written

b)
1. ▷ Jake was kidnapped by the gangsters.
2. ▷ The loot had been hidden in the tunnel (by Gerry).
3. ▷ The criminals were arrested (by the police) and the bullion was found.
4. ▷ Maybe Ray will be given a small reward by the insurance company / Maybe a small reward will be given to Ray by the insurance company.

C.
1. ▷ red-handed
2. ▷ punishment
3. ▷ adventure

D. – –

solutions to the worksheets — Ch. 1

A.
1. ▷ He had been waiting for his exam results.
2. ▷ She had promised to buy him a return air-ticket to anywhere in the world.
3. ▷ He has not seen him for 16 years / He last saw him 16 years ago.
4. ▷ He wants to travel to Australia.
5. ▷ She is not very happy, but she has accepted his decision.
6. ▷ He wrote that he was travelling to Australia and would like to stay with him.
7. ▷ He worked in a factory.
8. ▷ He sent an old picture Alex had drawn when he was two years old.
9. ▷ He remembered the past when he and his parents were still together.

solutions to the worksheets — Ch. 2

A.

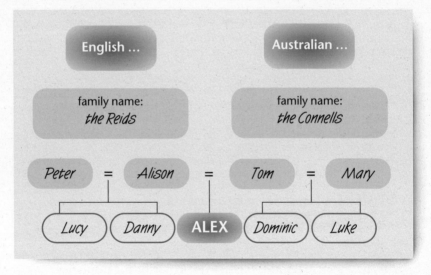

B.
1. He cared for his step-father, who had always been good to him, so he felt a little guilty about leaving his English family to visit his real father.
2. She told him that his father was in London, and that he was often there.
3. He was angry because his father had never tried to contact him when he was in London.

4. They went to the beach.
5. Her name is Dani Klavans. She is a beautiful girl, who lives next door to the Connells and she plays the keyboards in a pop group.
6. On the first evening he went to a concert of Dani's group, the Beat Crew. The next evening he himself played the guitar with the group at their concert.

C.

1. ▷ confused
2. ▷ departure lounge
3. ▷ impressed

solutions to the worksheets — ch. 3

A.

The next morning Mary told Alex that his father wouldn't be back before the 17th. She suggested that Alex should visit her brother in Adelaide and meet her nephew Kevin. Everything was arranged and Alex went to Adelaide by coach. On the way he got an impression of the vastness of the continent. In Adelaide he was met by Kevin. The two boys liked each other from the beginning.

The next day Kevin and Alex went to Kangaroo Island. Alex thought it was wonderful there. He especially liked all the wild animals which were not frightened of people. At the campfire he wrote a postcard to his parents in England. The boys stayed there for four days.

After a short stop in Adelaide they left for Wilpena Pound. As they drove north, the land became drier and drier, as they travelled into the "Outback". They saw ghost-towns and caves with Aboriginal paintings. They left early the next day to climb one of the highest mountains. This took them four hours. From the top they had a fantastic view, but on the way down they got soaked to the skin from a heavy downpour.

Alex was very angry with his father, because he had learnt from Kevin that Tom hadn't told Kevin that he had been married in England and had a son there. He was so annoyed that he did not care any more if he saw Tom in Sydney or not. But finally he did take the coach back to Sydney.

solutions to the worksheets — ch. 4

A.

1. ... he was going to meet Tom.
2. ... had had to go away again and was in Singapore.
3. ... play in the band in Melbourne.
4. ... played several gigs / gave several concerts and appeared on TV.

5. ... kissed for the first time.
6. ... Alex thought it was not pleasant to disturb the penguins with the lights.
7. ... meet on Thursday, either at home or at Sabrina's bar.

▶ **B.**

1. ▷ grinning
2. ▷ drizzle
3. ▷ race
4. ▷ nod
5. ▷ stage
6. ▷ hectic schedule
7. ▷ suntan oil
8. ▷ melts

▶ **C.**

1. ▷ a lot of time
2. ▷ bright light that helps the audience see the performers
3. ▷ to lose one's way / not to know where one is
4. ▷ the place in a hotel where you get your keys and pay your bill
5. ▷ to have a lot of things to do
6. ▷ when you know somebody or something quite well

▶ **D.**

▷ drums
▷ electric/bass guitar
▷ saxophone
▷ keyboards

✱ **E.** – –

✱ **F.** – –

solutions to the worksheets   *Ch. 5*

▶ **A.**

1. ▷ The journey back was a nightmare.
2. ▷ The woman who helped them was Vietnamese.
3. ▷ They stopped in the Blue Mountains because the bus broke down.
4. ▷ While he was waiting for Terry to come, Alex wrote in his diary.
5. ▷ The mechanic wanted two hundred dollars for putting one wire back into place.
6. ▷ When Alex saw his father in the audience he got shaky fingers.

▶ **B.**
1. ▷ bike (it does not have a motor; it only has two wheels)
2. ▷ puncture (not a car part)
3. ▷ on time (the others all have to do with being late)
4. ▷ painter (has nothing to do with a pop concert)

solutions to the worksheets   *ch. 6*

▶ **A.**
1. ▷ Right.
2. ▷ Tom made a lot of jokes.
3. ▷ Right.
4. ▷ Right.
5. ▷ Wrong. Alex decided to go on a trip with Tom.
6. ▷ Right.
7. ▷ Wrong. During the trip Alex slept for some of the time.
8. ▷ Wrong. Once they had to stop because there was so much water.
9. ▷ Right.
10. ▷ Wrong. He felt like he had lost a father but gained a friend.

▶ **B.**

1.	the instrument that Alex plays	BASS GUITAR
2.	the people who listen to a concert	AUDIENCE
3.	when you have only got a mother	FATHERLESS
4.	area where there are lots of trees	FOREST
5.	Alex took one to Sydney	PLANE
6.	an Australian animal	KANGAROO
7.	when musicians are on a stage	PERFORMANCE
8.	another word for disagreement	CONFLICT
9.	Alex writes everything into it	DIARY

▷ C.

solutions to the worksheets   *ch. 7*

✹ A.
1. ▷ The sun was rising as/when Tom steered out of the harbour.
2. ▷ Gypsy Woman was a sailing boat which was 9 metres long.
3. ▷ After they had (had) breakfast, Alex lay back on the deck.
4. ▷ When Alex was diving he saw beautiful fish, which he thought was fantastic.
5. ▷ Tom told Alex to come out of the water because the sun was too hot.
6. ▷ When he went swimming and diving again in the afternoon, he felt very happy, until he saw what he thought was a shark
7. ▷ Although Tom was shouting for help, Tom only laughed because it was not a dangerous animal.
8. ▷ Although Alex had not been in real danger, he hated Tom for laughing at him.
9. ▷ On Whitsunday Island it rained heavily, which made everything wet – sleeping bags, towels, clothes – and washed away all their cooking utensils.
10. ▷ When Alex asked why Tom had left his family in England, Tom told him that he had been afraid of settling down and becoming an adult.
11. ▷ Alex, who understood what Tom meant very well, wrote in his diary again.

✹ B. – –

solutions to the worksheets — Ch. 8

A.
- On Whitsunday Island it was peaceful and quiet.
- Alex and his father spent the time swimming, snokelling, fishing and lying in the sun.
- The highway back to Sydney was noisy and crowded.
- Finally they arrived in Sydney.
- Mary told Alex that the band was expecting him the same evening.
- After a shower he went to the TV studio.
- Dani told him that they were at number one in the hit list.
- Their manager arranged a tour all over the country.
- Alex thought that his life was magical, like a fairy-tale.
- The group became a really big success.
- And Alex became a well-known person who was interviewed and who appeared in talk-shows.
- One day, after a long time, Alex and Dani were enjoying a free afternoon together at Byron Bay.
- From the lighthouse Dani showed him a group of dolphins in the water.
- They were his favourite animals.
- He realized that the dolphins were different because they were free.

B. – –

solutions to the worksheets — Ch. 9

A.
▷ Joe and Pete were always drunk and weren't able to play properly.
▷ They had their heads shaved and looked like skinheads which went against the image of the band.
▷ Trouble started between the skinhead fans and some immigrants at a concert.

- ▷ Their next single, a slow number, did not sell. The same happened with the next song.
- ▷ People forgot about the group.
- ▷ They were poor. Most of the money they had earned went to the manager

▶ **B.**
- ▷ On the one hand, he did not want to leave Dani. He still wanted to travel and not stay in one place. He liked Australia.

- ▷ On the other hand, he had promised his mother to come back to England and go to university. He needed qualifications for a future career.

✖ **C.** --

solutions to the worksheets — Ch. 10

▶ **A.**
- Alex had a long talk with Tom about his future.
- Alex left Australia and went back to England.
- Dani agreed to go with him.
- Dani began to study music in England.
- Alex and Dani called themselves The Dolphins and began to play music in local pubs.
- Alex decided not to change his surname.

✖ **B.** --

✖ **C.** --

✖ **D.** --

solutions to the worksheets

Ch. 1 Betrayed

▶ **A.**

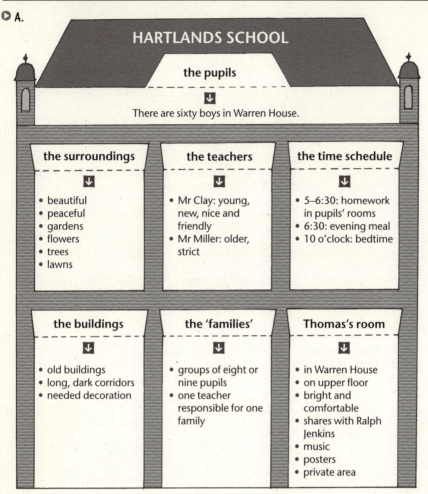

❋ **B.**

1. They live abroad and are quite wealthy, as they can afford to send their son to boarding school and have an expensive car.

2. Students might consider the following: She had chosen the school, she hardly spoke to Thomas and never asked about this thoughts and feelings. The fact that she embraced him came as a surprise.

3. --

❋ **C.** --

solutions to the worksheets — Ch. 2

A.

1. At 10 o'clock John Clay heard pupils shouting and running in and out of the their rooms, toilets flushing, water taps running and doors banging open and shut.

2. When he heard a military voice and a whistle, he wanted to meet the man who had so much authority.

3. At 11 o'clock Mrs Winterton asked him to go downstairs because there was a lot of noise coming from one of the rooms.

4. When Clay went into the room, he found a group of older pupils who were watching TV and who had been smoking.

5. The pupils only left the room when Mr Miller arrived and ordered them to go to their own rooms.

6. Miller told Clay that he had been at Hartlands for 40 years.

7. Miller told Bradley that he had to help him paint the fences around the tennis court.

B.

Two of the older boys came upstairs after midnight. They filled a large plastic sack with water, burst into Thomas's room and poured all the water over him, as he was lying in bed. Thomas, his bed and the floor were very wet.

C. --

D.

1. gym
2. dormitory
3. wardrobe
4. locked
5. complain
6. turn it down
7. envy
8. towel

E. --

solutions to the worksheets — Ch. 3

A.

1. ▷ During the meal it is very noisy. After the meal there is a gong and the headmaster makes a speech. Then the pupils can make some announcements for the day. Finally, the names of the pupils who have received post are read out. While the others leave the room, they go to a table where they stand in a line to collect their letters.

2. ▷ He expects them to accept and respect the rules that the teachers and pupils have agreed on. One of them is not to throw cold water on new pupils.

3. ▷ He thinks he is probably the worst pupil at the school. He suspects him to be at the bottom of a lot of nasty things that happen at Hartlands, but Bradley is able to escape punishment because somebody else always covers up for him.

B.

1. ▷ How did Mr Graham speak?
2. ▷ What did Mr Clay think when he looked at Thomas?
3. ▷ What did Bradley do during Mr Graham's speech?
4. ▷ How long had Mr Hansen been at Hartlands?
5. ▷ Why hadn't the headmaster thrown Bradley out of the school?
6. ▷ What did the younger pupils ask Mr Clay to do?

solutions to the worksheets — Ch. 4

A.

Yes	No
bossy; impertinent; threatening;	cheerful; friendly; shy; nervous;
intimidating; a bully;	frightened;
self-confident; rude; arrogant; strong	honest; fair; gentle; loud; timid

To be discussed: helpful; polite; a good friend; respectful; thoughtful; coward

solutions to the worksheets — ch. 5

A.

Come to our school pub!!!

Open every evening

from _seven_ till _ten o'clock_

Here you can _be alone, play your own music and sit and talk to your friends. We serve non-alcoholic drinks, of course._

The atmosphere is _nice and comfortable_.

You can have a great evening at the Hartlands Pub.

You don't have to _go into town_ to enjoy yourself.

The Pub Team

B.

1. ▷ The teachers suspect that he earns quite a lot of money and puts it in his own pockets. They think he runs a private business, as he is the person who buys the drinks, fixes the prices, checks the money, chooses and pays the barmen.

2. ▷ Bradley's father is a rich businessman, probably the owner of a firm. He is used to giving orders. He drives a large impressive car. He behaved arrogantly when he went into Mr Richards's office without being announced.

3. ▷ He wanted to stop the public inquiry which was to be held into his son's organization of the school pub.

4. ▷ He always liked to do things for his old school; he thanked Mr Richards for the private lessons he had given to his son; he invited Mr Richards and his wife to dinner; he sent men to install Mr Richards's new kitchen; he mentioned that it was the parents who financed the school and so they should decide how it is organized; he believed Mr Richards should be the next headmaster.
He did everything to influence Mr Richards and made it clear that he had a lot of influence which he might use in the school. Mr Richards was obviously impressed by Mr Bradley as he allowed himself to be dominated by him.

C. — —

solutions to the worksheets — Ch. 6

A.

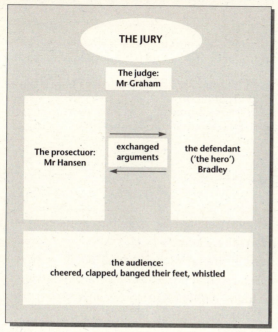

B.

Mr Hansen's arguments:

- the pub cannot be a private business
- Bradley makes huge profits (hundreds of pounds)
- it is the school that pays for all the expenses (rent, electricity, furniture)
- there are no receipts, no documents

Bradley's arguments:

- he has a lot of expenses and makes hardly any profit
- he pays the people who work there
- he pays for the music, the equipment, the damage, the decorations
- he alone runs the risks
- he has documents that can be checked

C.

1. – –
2. ▷ A committee of teachers and pupils will be formed to check the money and the number of drinks that have been sold in the pub every day.
3. ▷ They might have come from Mr Richards or they could have been put together by friends of Bradley.
4. ▷ On the one hand, it is very democratic, as everyone can see what happens. On the other hand, it is like a huge show.

solutions to the worksheets — ch. 7

A.

1. One afternoon John Clay walked to the ruin, which was on the top of one of the hills near the school.
2. When he arrived, he thought he was alone, but he wasn't.
3. After Mr Clay realized that it was Thomas Walker, he went over to him, but he found it difficult to start a conversation, because it was not a normal school situation.
4. Mr Clay apologized for not having enough time for the quieter pupils.
5. He realized that there was a secret world in the dormitories, which was hidden from the teachers and was full of violence and power.
6. When they walked back to the school grounds, they saw Bradley, who was sitting in a large car.
7. Although Mr Clay was very friendly to the boy, Thomas did not want to say anything about Bradley.
8. In the office a policeman informed Mr Clay that they had caught a pupil who had been riding too fast on a motorbike and did not have any papers, which was a serious offence.

B. – –

C.

1. ▷ He was breathing heavily. (p. 47, ll. 30f.)
2. ▷ Time goes by so quickly. (p. 48, l. 30)
3. ▷ Thomas shrugged. (p. 48, l. 33)
4. ▷ I might be able to go and live with her in Switzerland. (p. 49, ll. 10ff.)

solutions to the worksheets — Ch. 8

A.

1. W. He acted very casually and self-confidently.
2. W. He said it was Peters's problem.
3. R.
4. W. He said he could use Thomas as an informer.
5. N. We don't know whether Bradley sent them.
6. W. Everybody would think that the boys were playing.
7. R.

B. — —

C.

Thomas	John Clay	Bradley	Bradley's friends
• frightened	• a bit nervous	• inconsiderate	• violent
• hurt	• serious, but not too strict	• self-confident	• a gang
• a victim	• kind	• a good athlete	• cowardly
• isolated	• helpful		• cruel

D.

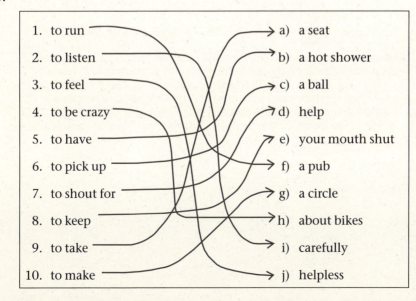

1. to run → c) a ball
2. to listen → h) about bikes
3. to feel → j) helpless
4. to be crazy → h) about bikes
5. to have → b) a hot shower
6. to pick up → d) help
7. to shout for → d) help
8. to keep → e) your mouth shut
9. to take → a) a seat
10. to make → g) a circle

solutions to the worksheets — ch. 9

A.

1. ▷ Mr Hansen
2. ▷ pupils
3. ▷ not enough discipline
4. ▷ dismissing some of the people who worked at the school

B.

1. ▷ He wants the pupils to feel happy and enjoy an open and friendly atmosphere. They should learn to help each other. (p. 61, ll. 22–28)

2. ▷ The person who was last given a work contract should be the first to be dismissed. At Hartlands that would be John Clay.

3. ▷ On the one hand, he has his idea of what a school could be like. On the other hand, he feels the pressure of the difficult financial position. Some of the parents want more discipline and the school is losing pupils, which means the school is losing money.

4. ▷ What had Thomas told Mr Clay?

C.

The school trustees met in the headmaster's office because they were worried about the financial situation of the school. The school had been losing some of its pupils and there wasn't a long waiting list of parents who wanted to send their children to the school. Although there were some letters from worried parents, Mr Graham believed the majority of parents were happy with the way the school was run and felt that their children were in good hands.

However, the trustees, while not wanting to return to stricter methods, wanted to see some changes. After studying the costs from all sides, they had come to the conclusion that the headmaster should reduce the number of people employed by the school.

Mr Graham was shocked at the suggestion. He looked down at the papers on the table and felt that everything had been reduced to numbers, that everything was seen in the form of profit or loss.

He breathed in deeply and pushed his chair back from the table and suggested that they take a break.

Later he would have to look at the contracts and then decide who he should fire.

solutions to the worksheets — ch. 10

A.

1. …he was thinking of what Thomas had told him and of what would happen next.

2. … the light in Dexter's room.

3. … called a special teachers' meeting for the next morning … come to the evening meal.

4. … Hansen and Clay went into the school building.

5. … stopped in front of Dexter's room.

6. … that a party was going on.

7. … on the door … that the pupils had to open the door or he would break it open.

8. … there were some boys and a girl from town in Dexter's room; they were all drinking and smoking.

9. … was a fridge.

10. … was lying under the bed and could not help sneezing.

11. … out of the fridge and threw it at Dexter, who ran out of the room with it.

12. … to follow him.

13. … were the winners; the teachers had no proof that the pupils had done anything wrong.

B.

1. ▷ soweit ich weiß
2. ▷ Haben Sie eine Ahnung, worum es dabei geht?
3. ▷ Da hast du Unrecht.
4. ▷ Ich konnte nichts dafür.

solutions to the worksheets — Ch. 11

A.

Mr Graham

- We have got information but no proof.
- Bradley has confessed that he had drugs in his room and has given the names of some of the drug dealers in town, so he is being cooperative.
- He is leaving the school at the end of the year anyway. We have got serious financial problems and Bradley's father has always been very generous to the school.
- The fact that Mr Clay hit Bradley in front of the other pupils puts him in the wrong.

Mr Hansen

- Bradley has committed a serious crime. He must be punished and handed over to the police.
- We know that he has drugs in his room as well as alcohol.
- We know that we cannot believe what Bradley says.

▶ **B.**

✱ **C.**

1. Yes. The deal was that Mr Graham would keep Bradley at school if Bradley gave him information about young people from the town. Nothing about drug dealing at Hartlands would be made public. Bradley probably promised to take no action against Mr Clay for hitting him.

2. – –

3. The school needed to save money and they were the two newest teachers, as well as those causing the most problems for the headmaster.

▶ **D.**

Hansen said that what Bradley had done / did was a serious crime and that Mr Graham should hand him over to the police, as he belonged in prison. That was the only place where he would realize how many mistakes he had made.

    The headmaster reminded Mr Hansen that he had no proof. They only had Bradley's own words as he had confessed and told them what he knew if he could have one last chance.

    Mr Hansen accused Mr Graham of doing / having done a deal with Bradley. They were covering up and letting Bradley walk away free.

▶ **E.**

1. If we keep Bradley at our school, we can/will avoid a scandal.

2. If he fails his A-levels at the end of the year, he will have to leave the school.

3. If we keep all the teachers here, we will have a large deficit.

4. If the press finds out about the drugs, there will be a big scandal.

5. If you give me any concrete proof of Bradley's drug dealing, I will take him to the police.

F. --

solutions to the worksheets — Ch. 12

A. More questions!

1. He came to beat him up for informing Mr Clay of Bradley's drug dealing.

2. He probably wanted to show that Bradley had not changed, and that Bradley had won.

3. --

B.

Hansen froze. His eyes widened. The colour left his face (p. 74, l. 17). His heart sank and he felt himself tremble with fear … Thomas's knees began to shake and his throat felt dry. (p. 75, ll. 12–15)

C. --

D. --